ZOO ANIMAL MYSTERIES

A Cheeky Chiller

by Alyse Sweeney

Consulting Editor: Gail Saunders-Smith, PhD

Consultant: Jackie Gai, DVM
Zoo and Exotic Animal Consultant

CAPSTONE PRESS
a capstone imprint

Pebble Plus is published by Capstone Press,
151 Good Counsel Drive, P.O. Box 669, Mankato, Minnesota 56002.
www.capstonepub.com

072011
006231CGVMI

 Books published by Capstone Press are manufactured with paper
containing at least 10 percent post-consumer waste.

Library of Congress Cataloging-in-Publication Data
Sweeney, Alyse.
  Cheeky chiller : a zoo animal mystery / by Alyse Sweeney.
     p. cm.—(Pebble plus. Zoo animal mysteries)
  Includes bibliographical references and index.
  Summary: "Simple text and full-color photographs present a mystery zoo animal, one feature at a time, until its identity
is revealed"—Provided by publisher.
  ISBN 978-1-4296-4499-0 (library binding)
  1. Chimpanzees—Juvenile literature. I. Title. II. Series.
  QL737.P96S97 2011
  599.885—dc22   2010001348

Editorial Credits

Jenny Marks, editor; Heidi Thompson, designer; Svetlana Zhurkin, media researcher; Eric Manske,
     production specialist

Photo Credits

Alamy/Elvele Images, 19; Norman Tomalin, 10–11, 13
Corbis/Gallo Images/Martin Harvey, 15
Getty Images/Photographer's Choice/Jean-Marc Truchet, 4–5; Photolibrary/Clive Bromhall, 17; Photolibrary/Kristin
     Mosher, 9
iStockphoto/Brandon Laufenberg, cover
Nature Picture Library/Karl Ammann, 7
Shutterstock/Tiago Jorge da Silva Estima, 21

Note to Parents and Teachers

The Zoo Animal Mysteries set supports national science standards related to life science. This
book describes and illustrates chimpanzees. The images support early readers in understanding
the text. The repetition of words and phrases helps early readers learn new words. This book
also introduces early readers to subject-specific vocabulary words, which are defined in the
Glossary section. Early readers may need assistance to read some words and to use the Table of
Contents, Glossary, Read More, Internet Sites, and Index sections of the book.

Table of Contents

A Forest Mystery 4

Fingers and Toes 14

Mystery Solved! 20

Glossary 22

Read More 23

Internet Sites 23

Index 24

A Forest Mystery

This book is full of clues

about a mystery zoo animal.

And the animal is me!

Can you guess what I am?

Here's your first clue:

In the wild, you'll find me

in African rain forests.

■ **Where I Live**

North America

Europe

Asia

Africa

South America

Australia

Antarctica

Every day I build

a new nest in the treetops.

I bend leafy branches

to make a soft bed.

I'm an omnivore. That means
I eat both plants and animals.
I search the ground and trees
for fruit, leaves, seeds,
and insects.

Sometimes my thick black hair

gets full of dirt or bugs.

Luckily I live in a community.

Grooming one another's hair

keeps us clean and happy.

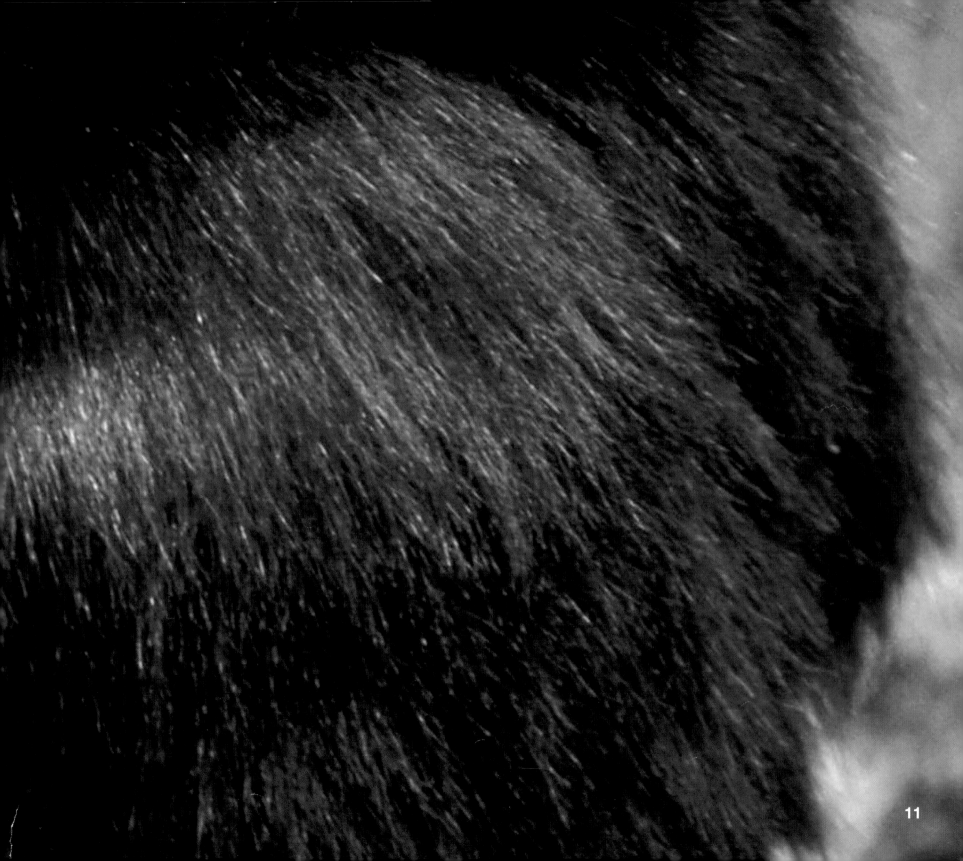

My community is friendly and playful. We say "hi" with a kiss or hug. We wrestle and chase each other through the trees.

Fingers and Toes

I have a big toe

on each foot. Do you?

My long toes help me

hold on to branches

when I climb.

My hands have thumbs,

like yours do.

I can grip tools

with my fingers and thumbs.

Do you smile

when you are happy?

I do too!

When I grin, I show

only my lower teeth.

Have you guessed what I am?

Mystery Solved!

I'm a chimpanzee!

This zoo mystery is solved.

Glossary

community—a group of 20 to 100 chimpanzees that live together

grip—to hold something tightly

groom—to stroke and clean hair

insect—a small animal with a hard outer shell, six legs, three body sections, and two antennae

rain forest—a woodland with lots of rainfall and very tall trees

thumb—the short, thick finger on each hand

tool—something used to make work easier

wrestle—to play by gripping or holding

Read More

Armentrout, David, and Patricia Armentrout. *Chimpanzees.* Amazing Apes. Vero Beach, Fla.: Rourke, 2008.

Pingry, Patricia A., and Chris Sharp. *Baby Chimpanzee.* San Diego Zoo Animal Library. Nashville, Tenn.: CandyCane Press, 2003.

Shores, Erika L. *Chimpanzees: Living in Communities.* The Wild World of Animals. Mankato, Minn.: Bridgestone Books, 2005.

Internet Sites

FactHound offers a safe, fun way to find Internet sites related to this book. All of the sites on FactHound have been researched by our staff.

Here's all you do:

Visit *www.facthound.com*

Type in this code: 9781429644990

Index

Africa, 4

chasing, 12

climbing, 14

communities, 10, 12

feet, 14

food, 8

grooming, 10

hair, 10

hands, 16

hugging, 12

kissing, 12

nests, 6

omnivores, 8

rain forests, 4

smiling, 18

teeth, 18

thumbs, 16

toes, 14

tools, 16

wrestling, 12

Word Count: 198
Grade: 1
Early-Intervention Level: 15